THE **Christopher Oill** FJH C

MW00680755

EARLY INTERMEDIATE

CHRISTMAS(ISH)

Witty and offbeat music for the holidays

by Christopher Oill

Notes from the Composer

Spice up your holiday recital with these humorous Christmas tunes! All good jokes have a setup followed by a punch line. So, when performing the pieces, speak the titles before playing, because the titles are setups, and the pieces are punch lines. Sometimes, as with "One Cookie Left Behind," you may wish to elaborate. ("Who left the cookie behind? How did it make you feel?") As a result, all of the giggling will surely put you and your audience into a joyous holiday spirit!

Christopher J. Oill

Christopher Oill

CONTENTS

FJH2351

TOO MUCH JOY

Joyously (♩ = ca. 92)

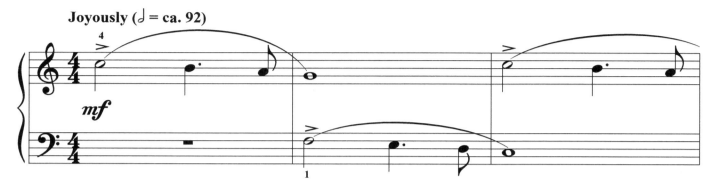

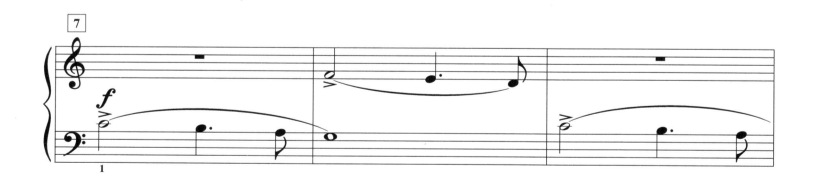

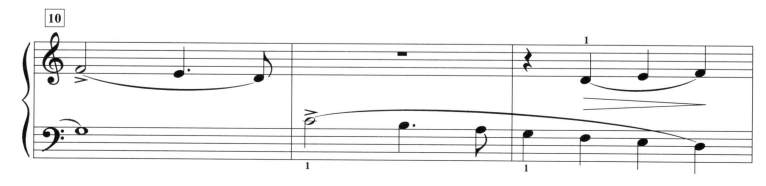

FJH2351

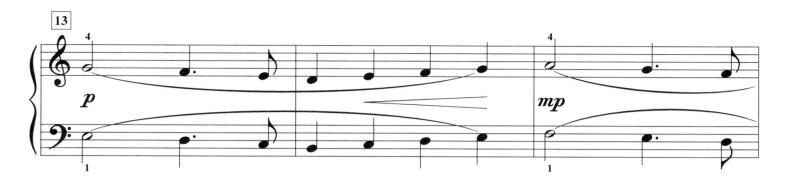

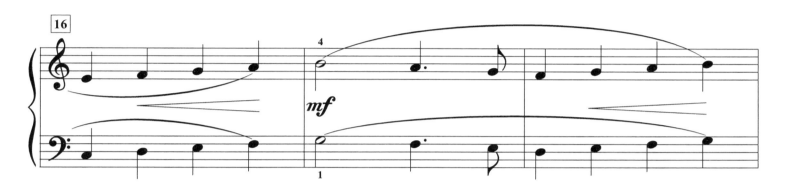

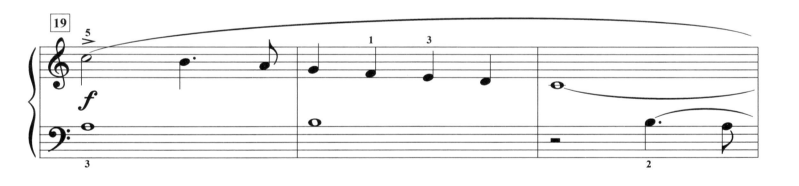

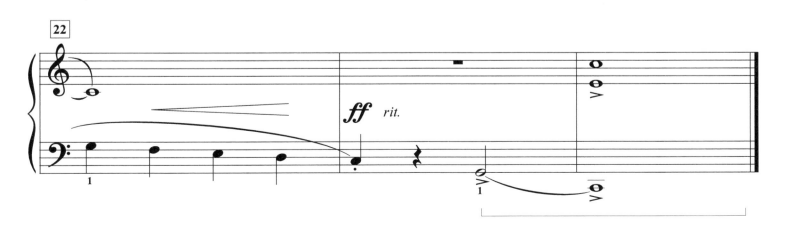

SNEAKY SANTA

Swift and sneaky ($\quad$ = ca. 108)

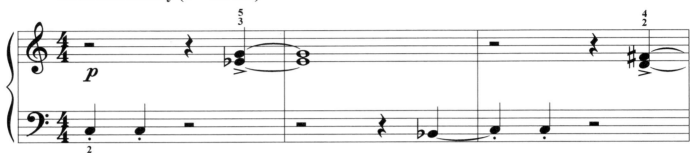

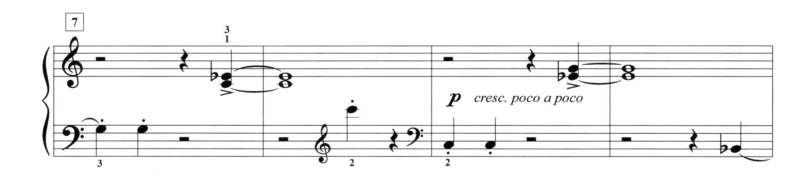

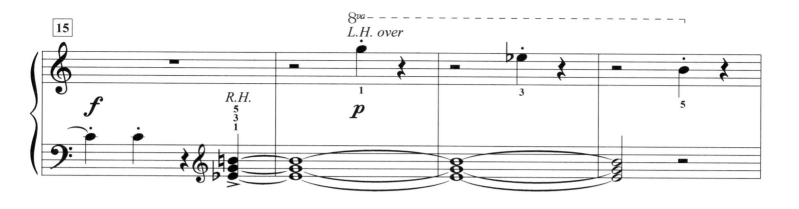

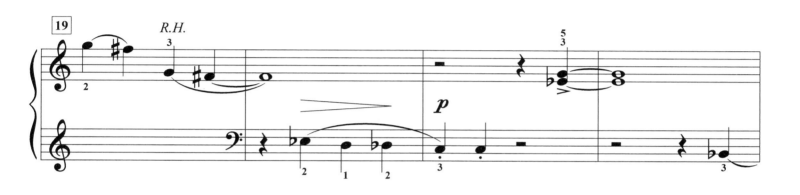

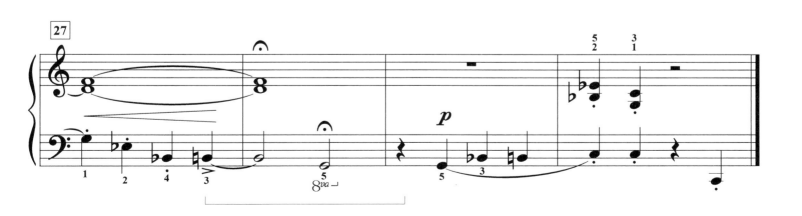

SILENT NIGHT

Instructions:

1. Pretend to begin playing, but don't.
2. Wait until the audience becomes slightly uncomfortable to end.
3. Relax and bow.

Seriously (♩ = 0)

pppp

SLIDIN' DOWN CHIMNEYS

With a cool, relaxed swing (♩ = ca. 92)

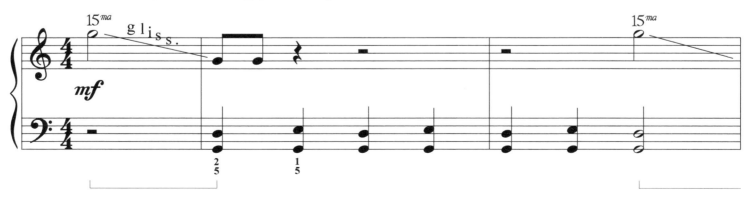

9

FJH2351

ELVES FALLING OFF SHELVES

Start slowly

An elf was sitting on a shelf.

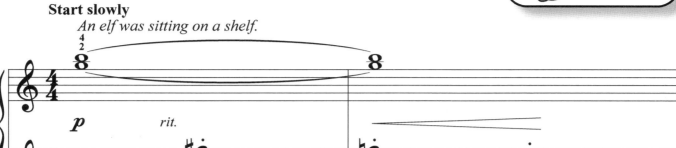

3 *He fell, crashing into many things.*   *He climbed back up with a friend.*

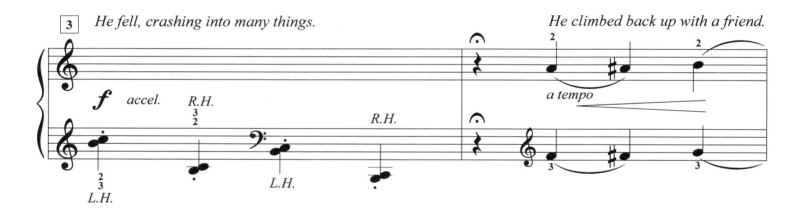

5   *They stopped on a lower shelf.*   *Uh-oh . . .*

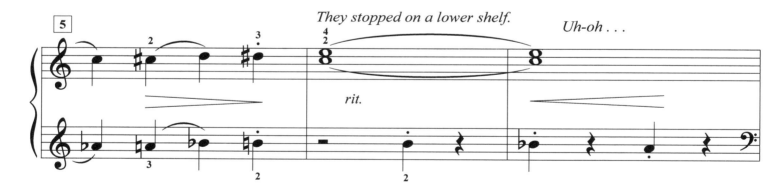

8 *They fell again.*   *They climbed to the higher shelf.*

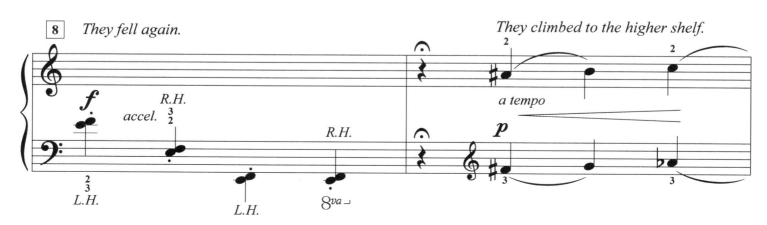

It took a long time . . .

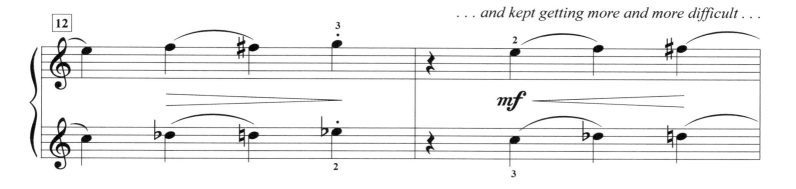

. . . and kept getting more and more difficult . . .

. . . but they made it!

Maybe they're safe?

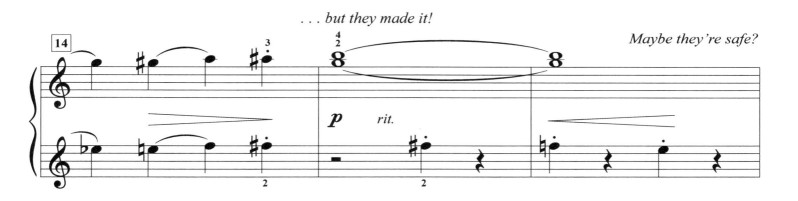

How frustrating!!!

Nope! They fell again.

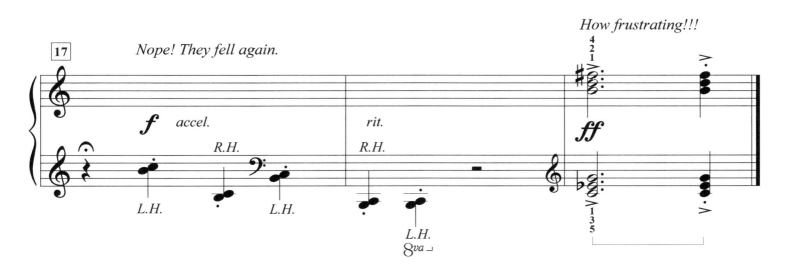

ONE COOKIE LEFT BEHIND

Passionately ($\quad$ = ca. 100)

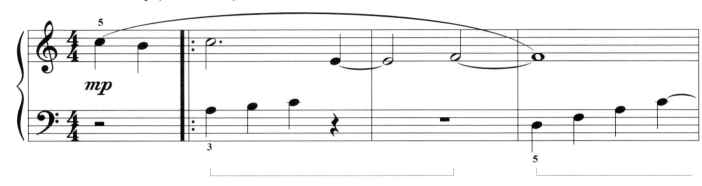

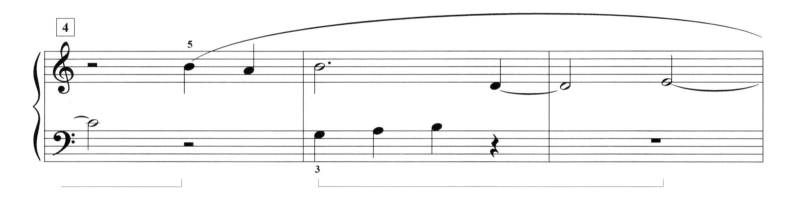

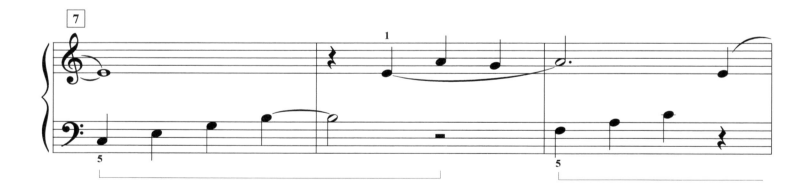

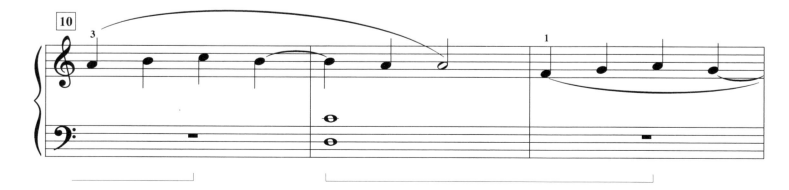

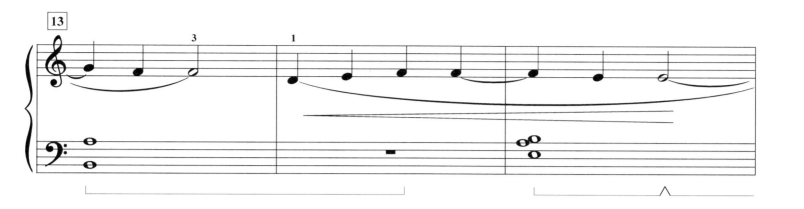

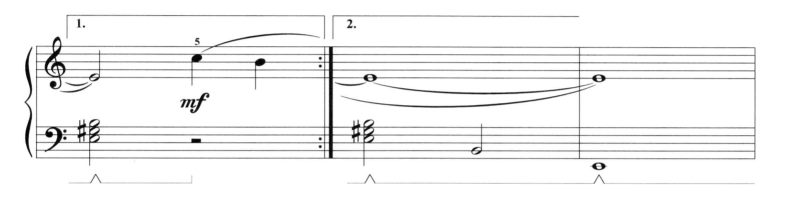

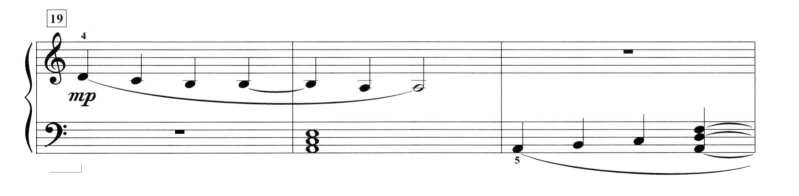

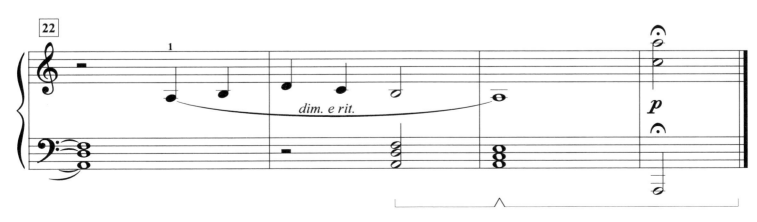

NOT ENOUGH LIGHTS FOR THE CHRISTMAS TREE

Quirky; light (♩ = ca. 120)

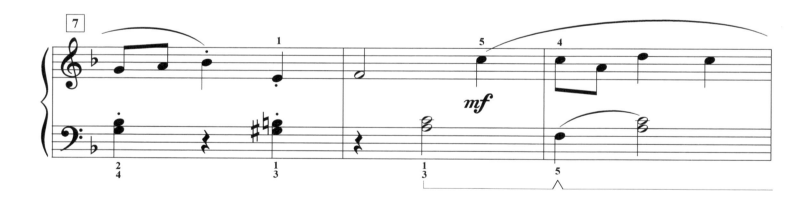

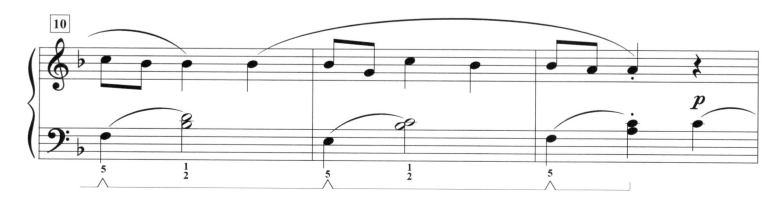

I GOT SOME MORE LIGHTS

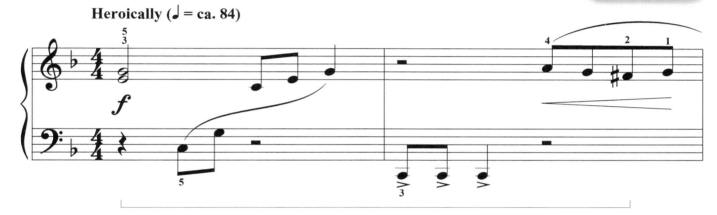

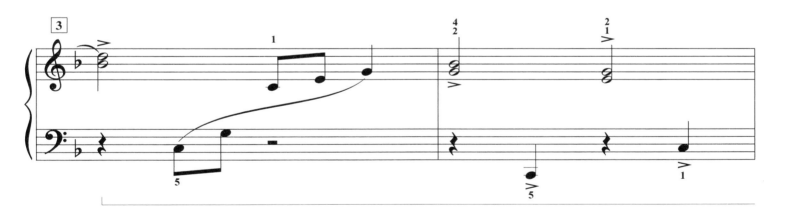

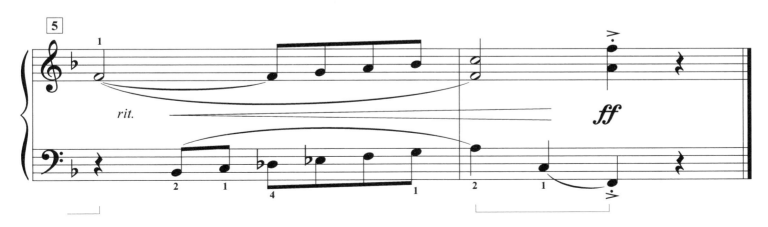

THAT SONG WITH THE FA-LA-LA'S

Confused, but cheerful (♩ = ca. 100)

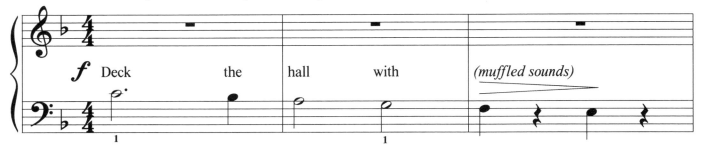

f Deck the hall with *(muffled sounds)*

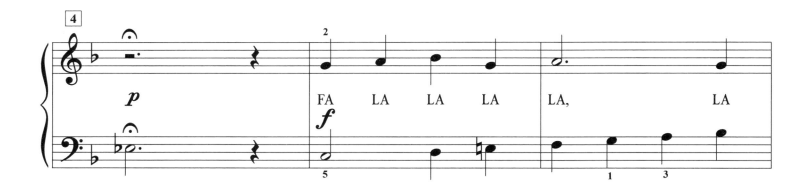

4

p

FA LA LA LA LA, LA

f

7

LA LA LA! 'Tis the

10

some - thing San - ta - Claus?

p

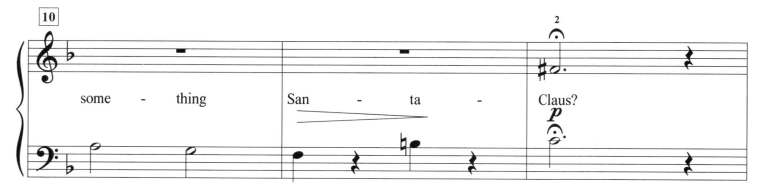

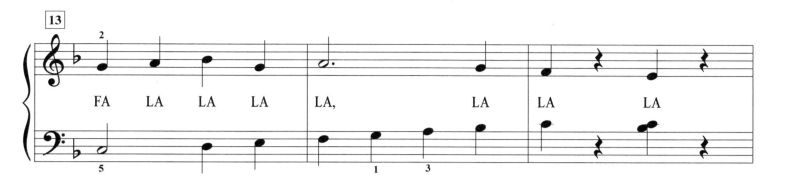

FA LA LA LA LA, LA LA LA

LA! Don, we know some

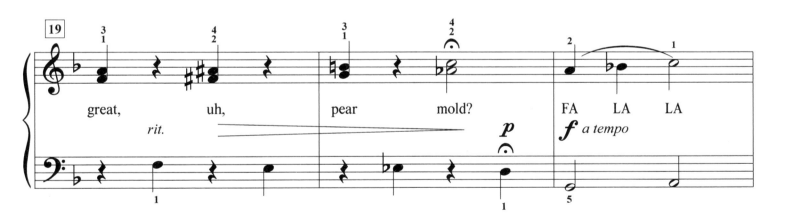

great, uh, pear mold? FA LA LA

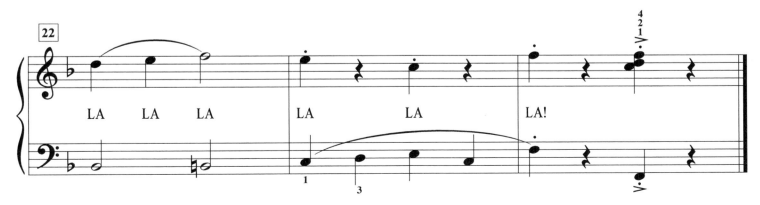

LA LA LA LA LA LA!

HARK!
MY PIANO'S OUT OF TUNE

Sweetly? (♩ = ca. 84)

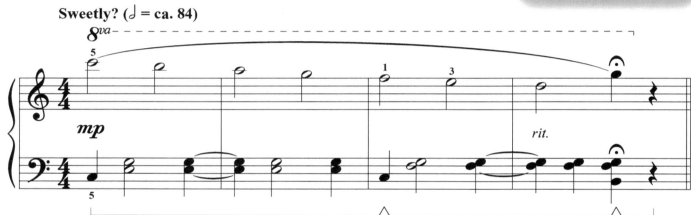

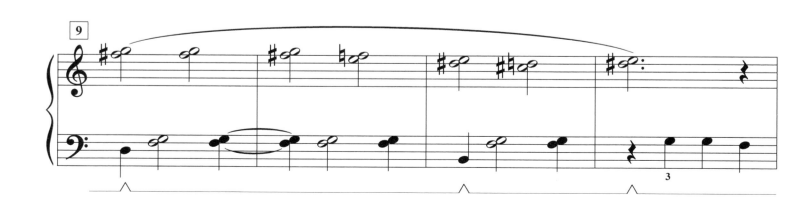

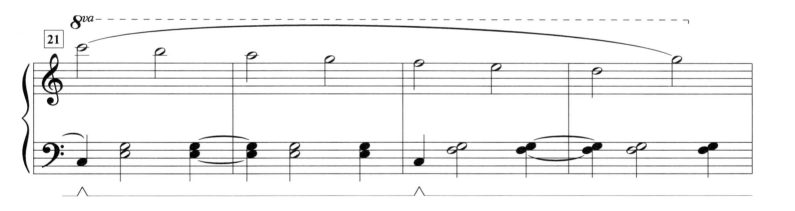

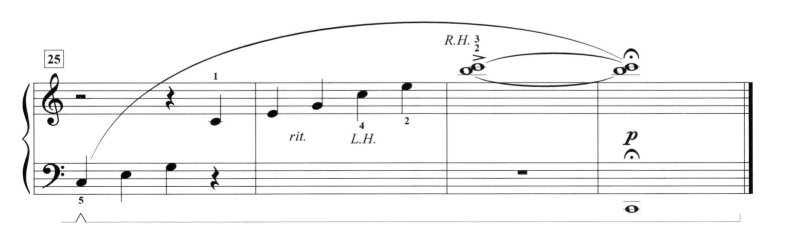

SANTA GOT PULLED OVER
FOR SPEEDING

Dangerously fast (♩ = ca. 180)

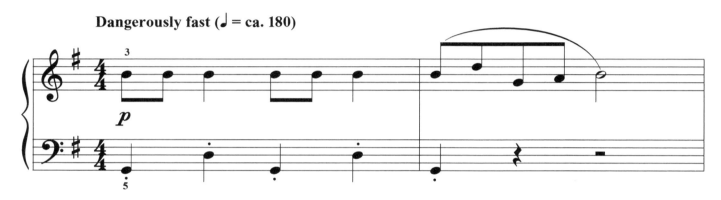

IT'S CHRISTMAS EVE, AND I CAN'T FALL ASLEEP

Restless; fast (♩ = 144-160)